500+ Hashtags for Writers

ELAINE L. ORR

DEDICATION

To everyone with the courage to put their words before the public.
May this book help you sell them.

500+ Hashtags for Writers
Elaine L. Orr

You are welcome to send hashtag suggestions,
to be included in future editions,
to elaineorr55@yahoo.com.

To learn more about Elaine's fiction, go to www.elaineorr.com.
The author has most used hashtags to market the Jolie Gentil Cozy Mystery Series

ISBN-13: 978-1500320553
ISBN-10: 1500320552

TABLE OF CONTENTS

STARTING TO USE TWITTER

Twitter (now X) was around for a few years before I started using it. I mentally ridiculed it. Who wants to communicate in 280-character spurts? In fact, I mostly don't. If I want to interact with people I know we use email or Facebook messaging or—heavens, how outdated–call or visit.

I wish I had not waited so long to use X to interact with people I don't know, mostly other writers and potential readers. For me, X has become a marketing tool, in the broadest sense. Most of my tweets are geared to selling my books, but they also let people know what I'm writing or that it snowed when I visited my brother near the Chesapeake Bay. No one cares about the latter, but I had a pretty picture.

It's not easy to say whether tweeting will help sell a book. You have to write a really good one, of course. I can say that I had no international sales until I started tweeting. I also had a two-week tweet hiatus during a move, and my sales went down. As a self-published author, I know my daily sales. If you have a publisher, it will be awhile before you get a royalty statement, so you probably won't know how tweets correlate to sales. Don't obsess over it, but spending ten minutes a day can't hurt. Tweeting should never be your only marketing tool.

What You Will Learn

This short book will tell you a bit about how to use X and provide lists of hashtags that deal with reading, writing, or selling books. There is a brief discussion on creating your own X following. That's good to do, but before you have thousands of personal followers you can reach lots of people with hashtags.

A hashtag is a way to send tweets to people who have similar interests. You can send to writers or readers by putting the pound sign in front of the terms: #writers #readers. A hashtag counts as part of the 280-character limit, but links to websites do not.

Hashtags are not case sensitive. I sometimes use capital letters to make it easier to read a hashtag.

You can find articles that define and explain hashtags in more detail. Wiki has a good one, or do a Google or Bing search. And remember, hashtags are used beyond X. You'll see them on Instagram, Facebook, TikTok, and more. They're also very democratic. Make up some new ones!

Your followers see tweets without hashtags, but it can be more effective to target a tweet to an audience that is more directly interested in what you are promoting. I write cozy mysteries (which I call murder without maggots), so I use tweets such as #cozymysteries and #parlorcozies. Readers see #cozies, but #cozy has a more general use in the hashtag world.

My Jolie Gentil cozy mystery series is set at the Jersey shore, so I also use phrases such as #beachread and #boardwalk. And #jerseyshore, of course.

Creating an X Account

If you do not have a X account, go to www.twitter.com and create one. It's not hard. Mine is @elaineorr55. People think I created it when I was 55, but five is a symbol optimists doodle. Color me an optimist. X will not let you create a name (called a X handle) if it is already taken.

You can also set up an account with your name and a X handle that is different than your name — and if your name is at all common it will be taken and you will have to do that.

An X name does not have to be your name, but if you are a writer it makes sense to let people find you on X. If you use a pen name that would certainly work, and if you write slapstick humor maybe the appropriate X name is @biggestdorkintheuniverse. Except it's too long, so you can't use it.

X has a number of Frequently Asked Questions (FAQs), some geared to new users, some to those with more experience.

Growing an X Following

The best way to have people follow you is to follow them. A good way to do that is to find people with interests similar to yours, and you can use hashtags to do that.

You check what a hashtag is geared to by going to the top right of your X page. There is a grey box for searches. Put in #mysteries and you'll see the kinds of tweets people send to #mysteries and also who sends those tweets. You can choose to follow some of those tweeters. They may follow you back.

X will suggest people for you to follow by displaying their names on one side of your screen. For two reasons, I click on a name before I follow. You can sometimes tell something from the X handle, but the profile might show something really different than you expect, and you don't want to follow them. Also, if the person has 2,000 follower and they follow only 20 people, they likely will not follow you back.

A popular hashtag is #F4F, which means if you follow someone they will follow back. That's fine, but you'll get a lot of followers with no interest in books, and sometimes people or groups you don't wish to associate with.

X enforces some kind of ratio of followers to follows, and if you get to a certain number of people you follow and few people have followed you back, you can't add more follows. No one knows the ratio, and the more followers you get the more X lets you follow. Delete some people you follow and then you can follow more.

There will always be people you want to follow who will never follow back, such as a TV show or publisher. Near the top of your X page you can see a link for Followers and one for Following. I periodically review the latter and delete those who have not followed back – unless I really want to see what they post.

I would absolutely stay away from new followers who say they gained 10,000 followers by doing…I'm not sure what. I have never clicked on one of these, and I've noticed that they no longer follow me after a couple of days of not following them.

Scheduling Tweets

My ten-minute-a-day tweeting schedule works well if my schedule is not crazy. However, it's not always orderly. If you will be away from your computer or traveling, it helps to have tweets scheduled to appear on the days you are gone. I used to use a third-party site, but X now has a scheduling function. Near where you click an icon to add an image to a tweet is a square icon that represents a calendar. Create a tweet, click the schedule icon, and it will be put out on the date you select.

Creating Tiny URLs

Web addresses are long, and who wants to look at a 50-character (or longer) link? You can now use one of several services to shrink them.

I use Bitly.
Another good one is TinyUrl.

There are others, but my author friends generally use these two. You will need to do a Google or Bing search to get to their sites. (See my blog post for the specifics.)

Because I'm placing this book at retail sites through the aggregator Smashwords, I cannot list any websites other than my own in this book. That used to annoy me, but I understand that if Apple is selling your book, they don't want links to Barnes and Noble in it (and vice versa).

However, you can get more specific info at my blog post https://elaineorr.blogspot.com/2022/01/shortening-web-addresses.html. I wish I could publish the shortened link here!

Bitly and TinyUrl have a free option. At Bitly, you can pay to tailor your Urls so they have your name or publishing company in each url. If you create a Url for a book on sale at Amazon, the tiny url will start with amzn.

The basic steps are:
1) Create an account
2) Click something that will say "Create" or "Add long Url."
3) Enter the long url
4) Press something that will say "Create Link" or "Continue."
5) Copy the link and enter it in a tweet or save it to a document on your computer.
6) Edit the link name if that is an option.

I edit all my shortened Urls so the list that Bitly automatically creates for me is easy to use. You could name them so they all start with the name of a site (Nook <u>Least Trodden Ground</u>) or start with the book name (which you would likely abbreviate (Least for Nook).

Let's Get to Hashtags

What follows are hashtags that can be useful to those who write books. Some are geared to genres, so if you don't write #historicalromances you won't use that hashtag. None of the hashtags deal with pornography or seriously violent and/or sadistic kinds of writing. If you write only that you may want your money back for this book. As adults we read and write what we want, but I don't care to help promote some kinds of writing.

It pays to check out what people tweet to a hashtag before you use it. For example #mysteryreader is geared to people who read mysteries to children. That may work for you, or it may not. I saw the hashtag #lookbook and thought it would refer to reading. It seems to relate to the fashion industry.

Many hashtags here are geared to specific genres. To help you think in subject-matter terms, I include some hashtags that relate to content rather than writing about content.

A lot of fiction books deal with hobbies, some deal with sports. You can do some research yourself to get more specific. For example, obvious ones would be #baseball, #football, and #basketball. If you have a book that deals with some historical aspects of a sport, you might use a hashtag such as #BabeRuth or #baseballhistory. Think about hashtags that might exist and search to see if they do.

Categorizing hashtags is not precise, so a hashtag may not be where you expect it in this book. One person will say something like #amishfiction should be in a general reading category. Another person will say, "I thought the only Amish fiction was the Harrison Ford movie." I put the general term in inspirational, then there's #amishromance, which is in Romance. Sorry, no #amishmystery, but there is @amishmystery.

Finally, there is sometimes the singular and plural of a word. For example, #author and #authors each have a lot of people associated with those hashtags. On the other hand, #mysteryreader would go to a fair number of people (who read mysteries to kids), but #mysteryreaders does not get used a lot. For the latter, you'll mostly see several authors who send tweets to it, including me. I no longer do.

On to the hashtags.

SPECIFIC HASHTAGS

Books and Readers, in General

#amreading

#avidreader

#bestsellers

#bookalicious

#bookclub

#bookclubs

#booklist

#booklovers

#bookreader

#books

#booksbymen (There is no hashtag for this as of spring 2014, but think how much trouble I'd be in if I put one sex here but not the other.)

#booksbywomen

#booksinprint

#bookstoread

#bookworm

#boxedset (multiple books for one price)

#bynr (for be your next read)

#fiction

#firstedition

#fridayreads

#goodbooks

#Goodread (a book someone likes)

#Goodreads (the book website)

#greatread

#hotread

#LitChat

#lovebooks

#mustread

#newbooks

#nonfiction

#novel

#novella

#novellas

#novels

#paperbacks
#popularfiction
#Pulitzer
#PulitzerPrize
#quickreads
#read
#readers
#readersfavorite
#reading
#readinglist
#readthis
#vintagebooks
#wattpad (unlimited stories)
#weekendreader
#weekendreads
#whatareyoureading
#whattoread

Writers, in General

#author
#authorinterviews
#authors
#Authorship
#authortools
#fictionwell (essays on writing literary fiction)
#novel
#IAN
#poets
#reviews (more than books)
#screenwriting
#WLC
#wordcount
#writingtips
#WritersCafe
#WritersLife
#WritersRoad
#WritersProblems
#WritingParty

#writinglife
#WritingCommunity
#writetip
#ShareTheLove4Authors

Audiobooks
#amlistening
#audible
#audio
#audiobook
#audiobooks
#acx
#booksontape
#lowvision
#narration

Bargain or Sale Books
#99C
#99cent
#99cents
#authorgiveaway
#bookaday
#bargainbooks
#bookdeals
#bookhaul
#bookoutlet
#cheapread
#kindleCountdowndeals
#writersrt

Book Festivals and Writers' Conferences
Some conferences have hashtags, some don't. These are good ways to find other writers and readers. Don't overuse them for book marketing. Only a few are mentioned here, a couple will guide you to more. If you're really looking for conferences in your area, do a Google or Yahoo search.
#bookfair
#bookfest
#mww22 www.midwestwriters.org

#nationalbook (National Book Award)
#writingconferences

Book Reviews or Related Site
#bookblogger
#booknerd
#bookreviewer
#bookreviews
#booktuber
#bookwhore
#LLbookreviews
#poetryreview
#reviews
#selfpublishingreview
If you want someone to review your books, do searches for things like book reviewers, book bloggers, etc.

Children
#booksforkids
#bookfunforkids
#children
#gradeschool
#homeschool
#kidlit
#kidlitart
#NewberyMedal (good place to look for books for kids)
#pblitchat (picture book lit chat)
#picturebooks
#preschoolers
#ReadingIsFun
#specialneeds (lots of good books for kids here)
#teacherslovefreestuff
#toddlers
#youngreaders
Many children's books are illustrated, so check out hashtags such as #illustration, #illustrator.

Ebook Markets

#amazonprime

#amazon

#Android

#apple

#barnesandnoble

#BN

#ereader

#ereaders

#Googlebooks

#Googleplay

#ibooks

#ipad

#iphone

#ipod

#itunes

#kindle

#kindlebook

#kindlebooks

#kindleebook

#kindleebooks

#kindlefire

#kindletouch

#kindleunlimited

#KDP

#KDPselect

#Kobo

#kobobooks

#mac

#newkindle

#Nook

#nookbooks

#Smashwords

#Smashwordsauthors (not used much)

#Sony (No longer has an ebookstore, but there are still Sony readers)

Family Focus

#brothers

#family

#familyfiction
#fathers
#fictionforthefamily
#grandfather
#grandmother
#mothers
#parents
#sisters
#twins

Fantasy

#comicart
#demon
#dragons
#epicfantasy
#fantasy
#fantasyfiction
#HarryPotter (kind of a cheat, but lots of fantasy readers here)
#magic
#urbanfantasy
#trilogy (This could go a lot of places; there are lots of fantasy trilogies.)
#vampire
#vampires

Free books

#free (not just for books)
#freeebook
#freebookoffer
#freeebooks
#freeforkindle
#freekindlebook
#freekindlebooks
#freereads
#kindlefree
#freeforkindle
#authorgiveaway

There are other hashtags geared to other ereaders, such as #nookfree and #kobofree. As of spring 2014, there were few entries for these hashtags.

Note to self: Implying that there are types of fiction geared to men or women could get you a lot of nasty comments.
Response from self #1: But some people want to market specifically to men or women.
Response from self #2: Grow a pair. (As a metaphor, this is gender neutral.)
Response from self #3: Consider therapy

Geared to Men
#fictionformen
#gaymen
#menshumor
#stayathomedad
#tweetsformen (little used)

Geared to Women
#AdmirableWomenWednesday (a shout-out to awesome, admirable women)
#chicklit
#fictionforwomen
#lesbianfiction
#stayathomemom (US)
#stayathomemum (UK)
#womensfiction
#womenwriters
#womenreaders

Hobbies
Many books deal with characters' special interests or hobbies, especially genre fiction. There are many other possible categories, and some could go in sports. The ones in this category are not team sports. There are dozens of other hobbies—look for those that relate to your book.
#artcollector
#campaignbuttons
#cooking
#crafts
#crossstitch
#familyhistory
#fishing
#genealogy (various spellings for this)
#horseriding
#hunting

#jogging
#knitting
#sewing
#shopping
#videogames (Not an easy place for this. Could be good for books for teens.)
#walking
#woodworking

Humor
#comedy
#comicbooks
#funnybooks
#humor
#indiecomics
#laugh
#laughing

Indie Pubs
#freelance
#IARTG (Indie Author Retweet Group, do join it)
#indies
#indieauthors
#selfpromosaturday
#selfpub
#selfpublishing

Inspiration
Some relate to religion, some do not.
#amishfiction
#believe
#betterlife
#ChristianFiction
#couragetochange
#feelgoodbook
#inspiration
#inspirational
#inspirationoftheday

#leadfromwithin
#livingthedream
#makingithappen
#spiritual
#truegrit
#twelvesteps
#writegoodnews
#yolo (you only live once)

Jolie Gentil Cozy Mystery Series
As an example of targeting your specific books
#appraiser
#beachread
#beachreadauthors
#boardwalk
#carnival
#cats
#dogs
#foodpantry
#friendship
#jerseyshore
#newjersey
#nj
#realestate
#reporter
#summerreads
#talklikeapirateday
You can see why these hashtags relate by going to www.elaineorr.com/Fiction.html

Kinds of Fiction (broadly defined)
Separate categories follow for some of these
#Fantasy
#HistFic
#HistNovels
#Horror
#literature
#literaryclassics
#literaryfiction
#mystery

#romance
#shortstory
#sciencefiction
#steampunk
#VSS (very short story)
#webfic

Marketing Books/Promotion

Some of these could appear in other categories.
#agents (as in good luck getting one)
#asmsg Stands for author social media support group. Join this free group before you use this hashtag. (www.asmsg.com)
#authorpi
#authortweetteam
#authorshostingauthors
#bestread
#biztalk
#blogger
#blogging
#bookblast
#bookbuzzr
#bookbuzzNYC
#bookmarketing
#bookplug
#bookplugs
#bookpromo
#bookpromotion
#bookseller
#booksigning
#booksofInstagram
#booksofTikTok
#bookstore
#bookstores
#BookTok
#booktube
#buyindie
#buymybook
#facebook

#FF (Stands for Friday Follow)
#FridayFiction
#goodkindles
#goodreads
#marketing (more than books)
#pressrelease
#promocave
#promoteyourbooks
#series (if you write one)
#webmarketing
#WritersHelpingWriters

Mysteries and Thrillers

#berkleyprimecrime
#coldcase
#cozies
#cozymysteries
#crimedrama
#crimefiction
#crimewriting
#CSI
#EdgarAward
#EdgarAwards
#edgars
#femalesleuth
#femalesleuths
#hardboiled
#murderstories
#mustreadmystery
#mystery
#mysteries
#mysterylovers
#mysteryreader (adults reading to children)
#mysteryseries
#mysterywriter
#mysterywriters
#NCIS
#pageturner
#parlorcozies

#suspense
#thriller
#womansleuth
#womensleuths

Nonfiction

Marketing for nonfiction is geared to the subject matter, such as #gardening or #baseball.
These are general ideas, and some nonfiction topics are good for marketing your fiction.
#biographies
#biography
#currentevents
#discovery
#farming
#memoir
#mindfulness
#selfhelp
#science
#travel
#vacation
Even more so than with fiction, the more specific a hashtag for nonfiction is, the better it helps
to sell a book. For example, if your book is about traveling in Greece, use #Greece but also
#Greekislands, #Greekolives, #Mediterranean

Paranormal

#astrology
#empath
#freakynight
#Future
#Horoscope
#medium
#paranormal
#paranormalactivity
#paranormalromance
#paranormalmystery
#nativeparanormal
#numerology
#psychic

#Supernatural
#wicca
#ZodiacSigns

Publishing

#cookbookstore
#digitalpublishing
#epublishing
#getpublished
#published
#publisher
#publishing
#romancepublishers
#selfpub
#selfpublishing
Use the name of your publisher or one that publishes the kind of books you write. People who like mysteries, for example, may look at #PenguinBooks.
#Harlequin
#HarperCollins
#Penguinbooks
#RandomHouse
#SimonSchuster
Look at the X handle to see what kinds of books they publish. These are two samples.
@OrionBooks
@wnbooks

Romance

#50shades (In case you wrote a similar book.)
#amishromance
#boyfriend
#Christianromance
#eroiticromance
#Harlequin
#historicalromance
#inlove
#love
#lovers
#mce (my crush everyday)
#NASCARromance

#paranormalromance

#Regencyromance

#romance

#romancefiction

#romancewriter

#romantic

#romanticsuspense

#RWA (Romance Writers of America)

#wedding

Science Fiction

#scifi

#syfy

#sciencefiction

#scifichat

#scififantasy

#StarTrek

#Trekkies

#StarWars

Special Use

This is a catch-all or sometimes-use category. I use these rarely. However, if I know a lot of people could see tweets with a hashtag, I may use it even if it does not directly relate to my book. Having said that, some of these could relate to your book and you may use them a lot. As a matter of principle, I don't tweet to disaster names. Because one of my books relates directly to Hurricane Sandy, I use that. Discretion, discretion, discretion. These will give you food for thought.

#AcademyAwards

#Christmas

#FathersDay

#GroundHogDay

#MothersDay

#Passover

#snowedin

#snowmageddon

#springbreak (almost no one uses this hashtag, which surprises me)

#TGIF

#throwbackthursday (Post old photos. Put one that relates to your book and include the link.)
#thankgoditsfriday
#weekend

Team Sports
Samples—there are dozens more. Use specific ones, such as 2014WorldSeries.
#americanfootball
#baseball
#basketball
#ESPN
#football
#hockey
#Lacross
#majorleagues
#rugby
#soccer
#superbowl
#swimming
#tball
#WorldSeries
#wrestling

Westerns
#cattle
#cattleranch
#Cowboys (or #cowboys)
#cowboystories
#farm
#JohnWayne
#LouisLamour
#oldwest
#ranch
#rurallife
#western (gets a lot more than books)
#westerns
#ZaneGray

Writers at Work
#AmEditing

#amrevising
#amwriting
#authorchat
#debutnovel
#firstdraft
#iamwriting
#newwriters
#novelists
#wordcount
#writingpact
#writingprompts
#writingquotes
#writersnight
#writersroad
#writersproblems
#writerchat
#writerscafe
#WritersLife
#writerslit
#WriterWednesday
#WW (Writer Wednesday)

Writing Careers

#advertising
#content editor
#copyediting
#copyeditor
#editor
#editors
#englishteacher
#fictionwriter
#freelance
#poet
#proofreader
#teacher

Young Adult and Middle Grades

In publishing, young adult is defined as ages 12 to 18, though it can include younger readers. New adult is a more recent term in publishing, and covers ages 18 to 25. That phrase is included here because kids tend to read above their age group.

#adolescents

#graphicnovel (includes many age groups, of course)

#MGlit (middle grade literature)

#middlegrades

#newadults

#teenfiction

#ya

#yalit

#YALitChat

#yaread

#youngadult

#youngadultlit

#youngadults

#youngadultbook

#youngadultbooks

Other ideas

Towns you live or lived in. I do #Ottumwa, #TakomaPark, #Muncie, #Springfield. Check the hashtag before you use it. On X, #Kensington (where I grew up) is the London neighborhood, not the Maryland town.

Basically, use any category to which you have a link. This could include schools you attended, high school sports teams you played on, or clubs you belonged to. Don't overuse personal connection hashtags -- there's only so much people want to know about your writing.

Will Retweet

You can ask friends to retweet for you, but they'll soon tire of being asked. Unless they have 10,000 followers who all like your books, it won' be effective anyway. There are people who out of the goodness of their hearts will retweet your book information. They will not tell you that they did a retweet, but you can click on Notifications on your Home page and they'll show. I send periodic thank-yous.

Your tweet is not sent as a request, just send a standard tweet to the retweeter's X addresses. One of the best ways to be retweeted is to do the same for others.

You will see ads for people who will send tweets for you, for a fee. I did a few of these when I first started tweeting, and usually paid $5. As I grew my own list of followers and learned how to use hashtags, I stopped doing this. I'm not saying don't do it. If you do, pick someone who tweets about books or reading.

I would absolutely stay away from your new followers whose profiles say they gained 10,000 followers by doing…I'm not sure what. I have never clicked on one of these, and I've noticed that they no longer follow you after a couple of days of not following them.

If your book is not free, don't send a request to those who retweet about free books.
Send tweets you hope to see retweeted to:

@authorkarma
@bookdealhunter
@booksandauthor
@booksffree
@BookYrNextRead
@ereaderperks

@freebooks

@FreeEbooks_4U

@FreeBookPromo

@Free_UK_eBooks (use a link for UK purchases)

@givekindlebook (Tweets when books are high on Amazon lists.)

@goodkindles

@IndAuthorSucess

@ibookstore

@IndBk

@KindleBookBlast

@kindleebooks

@kindle_promo

@kindle_free

@KindleFreeReads

@kindleswag

@MustReadMystery

@mystery_book (on day of publication only)

@mystwts

@nicekindle

@Retweets4Writer

@storyfind

@writeintoprint

CREATING, SENDING AND STORING TWEETS

This discussion presumes your tweets will largely be to promote books, but don't have only sales-oriented tweets. If your books are set in the countryside, have some with relevant photos. If your protagonist is a carpenter, occasionally tweet about making furniture.

The links you feature in tweets can get a reader to a site with multiple purchase options. This can be your web page or a page within a blog. You can also use links to individual sites, such as Amazon, Barnes and Noble, Google Play, Apple, Kobo, etc. Make sure to use shortened URLs.

Some retailers have different links for their sales points in different countries. Amazon has many, Kobo has the U.S. and Canada. If you want to call attention to Canadian readers, use that link and a relevant hashtag, such as #AmazonCanada or #KoboCanada.

You don't want to retype tweets. As you create tweets, save them in a Word document or other software so you can copy and paste them—not immediately, X won't permit that.

You'll probably create tweets for individual books or as a link to articles on your blog. Then copy them, using different hashtags.

I organize my list of tweets by book and blog post, and periodically weed out old tweets.

Happy tweeting!

Author Bio and Books

ABOUT ELAINE ORR

Elaine L. Orr writes four mystery series, including the twelve-book Jolie Gentil cozy mystery series. *Behind the Walls* was a finalist for the 2014 Chanticleer Mystery and Mayhem Awards. The first book in her River's Edge series, From *Newsprint to Footprints*, came out in late 2015, and the Logland series began with *Tip a Hat to Murder* in 2016. *Demise of a Devious Neighbor*, the second River's Edge book, was a Chanticleer finalist in 2017. Her newest series, the Family History Mystery Series, is set in the mountains of Western Maryland and debuted in 2020 with *Least Trodden Ground.* The second book in the series, The Unscheduled Murder Trip, received an Indie B.R.A.G. Medallion in 2021.

She also writes plays and novellas, including the one-act play, *Common Ground* published in 2015. Her novella, *Falling into Place*, tells the story of a family managing the results of an Iowa father's World War II experience with humor and grace. Another novella, *Biding Time*, was one of five finalists in the National Press Club's first fiction contest, in 1993. *In the Shadow of Light* is the fictional story of children separated from their mother at the US/Mexico border.

Elaine is a member of Sisters in Crime and the Indiana Writers' Center.

For a good overview of marketing books (which is so much more than social media marketing), I recommend Jeffrey Marks' *Intent to Sell: Marketing the Genre Novel,* which is in ebook, paperback, and audio.

No one will sell your books for you, so here's how you can find some of mine.
www.elaineorr.com
elaineorr55@yahoo.com
I also have a newsletter. Send an email if you'd like to be on it.

Jolie Gentil Series
Appraisal for Murder.
Rekindling Motives
When the Carny Comes to Town
Any Port in a Storm
Trouble on the Doorstep
Behind the Walls
Vague Images
Ground to a Halt
Holidays in Ocean Alley
The Unexpected Resolution
The Twain Does Meet (Novella)
Underground in Ocean Alley
Aunt Madge and the Civil Election (a long short story)
Sticky Fingered Books
Jolie and Scoobie High School Misadventures (prequel)
Boxed sets of the series are available as ebooks on all retail sites.

River's Edge Mystery Series
From Newsprint to Footprints
Demise of a Devious Neighbor
Demise of a Devious Suspect

Logland Mystery Series
Tip a Hat to Murder
Final Cycle
Final Operation

Family History Mysteries
Least Trodden Ground
The Unscheduled Murder Trip
Mountain Rails of Old

Other Fiction
Biding Time (YA Novella)
Falling Into Place (reflective fiction)
In the Shadow of Light (reflective fiction)
Secrets of the Gap (romantic suspense)

NONFICTION
Monett (Arcadia Publishing)
The Art of Deliberate Distraction
Words to Write By: Putting Your Thoughts on Paper
Writing When Time is Scarce – and Getting the Work Published
500+ Hashtags for Writers
Various Family History Books

Check out the index on Irish Roots Author, for articles on reading, writing, publishing, and whatever musings are going through Elaine's head.

www.elaineorr.com

www.ingramcontent.com/pod-product-compliance
Lightning Source LLC
Chambersburg PA
CBHW081409170526
45166CB00010B/3265